The Gardener's Scotland

Dawn MacLeod

DAWN MACLEOD started gardening at the age of four, assisting her father with week-end jobs at their home near London. The skill of a Highland grandmother with garden flowers added to the youthful enthusiasm. Pennies were spent at an adjacent nursery, whose proprietor—remembered as the exact counterpart of Beatrix Potter's Mr MacGregor—gave a handsome allowance of double daisies and pansies in return for his youngest customer's pocket money.

After Admiralty service in the Second World War she gave up a permanent post in London to help Mairi Sawyer at the famous gardens of Inverewe, Wester Ross; a happy companionship cut short by Mrs Sawyer's sudden death in 1953. Dawn MacLeod, who has designed and made several gardens, acknowledges help and inspiration gained from Mrs Sawyer and other well-known gardeners she has known, notably Vita Sackville-West (Sissinghurst), Margery Fish (East Lambrook) and Margaret Brownlow (Herb Farm, Seal).

In 1964 an interest in herb plants led to the work of initiating a herb exhibit at The American Museum, Bath, followed by election to the Council of the Society of Herbalists (now renamed The Herb Society). Her published books include *Oasis of the North* (Inverewe), *A Book of Herbs*, *Design Your Own Garden* and *The Gardener's London*.

Until 1977 the author lived in Berwickshire, and during the last six years has visited gardens all over Scotland.

Cover illustration: 'Cabbage palms' at Logan Garden

THE
GARDENER'S
SCOTLAND
Dawn MacLeod

WILLIAM BLACKWOOD
1977

First published in 1977 by
William Blackwood & Sons Ltd
32 Thistle Street
Edinburgh EH2 1HA
Scotland

ISBN 0 85158 118 8

Printed at the Press of
the Publisher

To my niece Gillian
a graduate of
the ancient University
of St Andrews

Contents

Illustrations

Preface

In her Wonderland, Alice found a bottle whose contents shrank her to keyhole dimensions.

In the wonderland of Scottish horticultural achievement I found no such potion, and have tried to fit an enormous range of material into this small book without the aid of magic.

The average garden-lover will be unlikely to regret my severe curtailment of plant names, especially long Latin ones. Those who cannot do without such detailed identification will obtain all they need, in regard to National Trust properties, from booklets on sale at the gates.

My plan has been to give space to one outstanding garden in each group, allowing for appraisal in depth, followed by shorter references to a number of others. Brevity should on no account be taken as a reflection on the excellence of those so treated. It is due solely to shortage of space.

It seemed essential to find room for mention of Scottish gardeners alongside the gardens they have made and tended. Quite by chance it appears that men and women have shared the honours equally.

Opening hours change from time to time, so it is not practicable to quote these. The National Trust for Scotland supplies up-to-date information about the properties it maintains, and the rest are for the most part covered by the booklet *Scotland's Gardens*; but there are other openings not related to the Scotland's Gardens Scheme—for example, Drummond Castle, whose garden has been open twice weekly in summertime. To discover these, newspapers and information offices should be consulted.   *Dawn MacLeod*

Acknowledgements

Thanks are offered to H.M. Queen Elizabeth The Queen Mother for graciously allowing access to her Castle of Mey and its garden; to Mr Sinclair who looks after it; the Earl of Ancaster; the Earl Cawdor, Elizabeth, Countess Cawdor, and Mr A. S. Wood; the Countess of Haddington; Sir Ilay and Lady Campbell; Flower, Lady Furness; Lady Mary Gilmour; Colonel A. N. Balfour of Dawyck and Mr Robert Blair; Mrs Betty Sherriff; Mrs Arthur Purvis.

To The National Trust for Scotland and Messrs J. E. Robson, W. R. Hean, R. D. Hillson, George Barron; the Regius Keeper, Royal Botanic Garden, Edinburgh, and Mr G. Kirkpatrick; Mr Eric Curtis, Curator, Glasgow Botanic Garden; The Royal Horticultural Society and Miss Elspeth Napier, Editor, *The Garden*; the General Organiser, Scotland's Gardens Scheme; Mr Jack Drake and Mr J. C. Lawson, Inshriach Alpine Nursery; Mrs V. M. Bethell, Aberchalder Alpine Gardens, and Mr Ewen MacDonald; Mr Alex Duguid, Edrom Nurseries; to Lord Horder for his slide of Pitmedden, and to Adam Tegetmeier for the black-and-white version.

In addition, to all those others who so kindly showed gardens which gave pleasure and lent perspective to this brief study, and to people who helped and encouraged the project, I am indeed grateful.

Dawn MacLeod

Backward Glances

ALTHOUGH the Roman occupation of Britain is usually held to mark the birth of gardening in England, it seems unlikely that the military excursions into Scotland allowed much opportunity for development of this peaceful and static art. With the coming of early Christian missionaries, there is fairly reliable evidence that horticulture was started by small religious communities. An eighteenth-century writer referred to the Abbey of Icolmkill (Iona) in the Hebrides, where traces of gardening could still be discerned, and a firmly established tradition suggests that nuns, who were settled on Iona from the thirteenth century until the Reformation, grew flowers in their cloister garth. A twentieth-century flower garden, planted there in 1923 when some restoration of ruined walls took place, commemorates both the earlier pleasance of the nuns and the late Mrs R. J. Spencer, whose family sponsored the work.

In such monastic records as have survived, there are references to gardens and orchards—the latter furnished in the main with apples and pears, some of which appear to have been extant at the beginning of the nineteenth century. Writing in 1813, Patrick Neill states that these fruits came into Scotland through religious leaders who were thoroughly conversant with the ideas of their counterparts in Europe. He mentions an apple called Arbroath Oslin, which he compares to the Burr-knot of England. Neither of these varieties is known to the modern apple-grower.

In the twelfth century David I of Scotland is said to have made a garden at the base of Edinburgh Castle, a somewhat unpromising site. George Chalmers in his *Caledonia Depicta* (1807) says that the Scottish nobles copied the royal example and continued the old monastic tradition by developing gardens and orchards on their own estates. Meanwhile ordinary folk had little chance of procuring such novelties, until the propagation of plants and trees in the gardens of great houses led to the release of surplus material, after which the cultivation of fruit and vegetables gradually spread and became popular.

By the seventeenth century, apples, pears, cherries gooseberries, currants and certain vegetables were being grown over a wide area of Scotland. Now that the country has become justly famous for its heavy crops of raspberries, it seems odd that this luscious fruit was not given prominence in writings of an earlier date. In his *Gleanings from Old Garden Literature* William Carew Hazlitt, a grandson of the famous essayist, makes a surprised comment on this point, saying that John Reid, author of *The Scots Gard'ner* (1683) 'does not say so much as might have been expected about the berry tribe, which has always been regarded as thriving northward better than in England'.

To return to orchard trees: in 1812 Dr John Walker wrote of a garden at Armadale in Skye belonging to the Macdonalds which contained good fruit and some very old trees. 'The first trees planted by art in Scotland were those of foreign growth, especially fruit-bearing trees. Long before the Reformation various orchard fruits, brought probably from France, were cultivated in the gardens of religious houses in Scotland.' In the City of Perth a street called 'Pomarium' still marks the site of an orchard which belonged to a vanished Carthusian monastery, and at the old house where Mary, Queen of

Scots stayed in Jedburgh are some venerable and highly picturesque pear trees, relics (it is thought) of monastic pomiculture. In 1934 the remains of a decayed tree, the famous 'Jethart Pear', supposedly put there by the ill-fated Mary, were removed and replaced with one planted by the late Queen Mary, consort of George V.

Melrose also was famous for its monastic orchards, mostly at Gattonside where good fruit is still produced. *The Agricultural Survey of Roxburghshire* (1798) reports that in 1793 two old trees at Melrose 'brought to perfection 60,000 pears—which sold for eight guineas in the market'. Patrick Neill mentions that even at the end of the eighteenth century there were still some very old trees, chiefly of French extraction, growing on abbey grounds. Many were of great size, several being thirty or forty feet high, with huge trunks and wide-spreading branches. One Red Honey Pear, between fifty and sixty feet high, had a trunk measuring nine feet in circumference. In the gardens of Cockenzie in East Lothian there used to be pears with the delightful names Jargonelle, Bergamot, and Greenpear of Yair. White and Carlisle Codlings, Hawthorndean, Summer and Winter Redstreaks, Nonsuch, Fulwood and Pippins are some names of apples cultivated at the time of the *Survey*.

The Earl of Buchan,* founder of the Society of Antiquaries of Scotland, was so pleased with his orchard at Dryburgh that he gave it the dignity of a Latin inscription:

'HOC POMARIUM, SUA MANU SATUM,
DAVID SENESCHALLUS BUCHANIAE
COMES, PARENTIBUS SUIS OPTIMIS PIE POSUIT.'

* David Steuart Erskine, 11th Earl of Buchan.

Honesty was no more common then than it is now, despite heavier penalties for culprits. The scarcity of fruit increased temptation to steal it when ripe, and guarding the precious crop required much vigilance. Apples and pears were often underplanted with gooseberries and currants, the berries being used in the main for home-brewed wine. The making of fruit-preserves with sugar did not occupy the cook's time until, in the tea-drinking eighteenth century, cane sugar was imported in quantity and gradually became cheaper. Now that the price has risen so steeply, together with the cost of dutiable wines, people are once again making their own fermented liquor at home, and cutting down on the jams.

At Achnacarry, in the Highlands of Scotland, the Chief of Clan Cameron owned the first 'kitchen garden' known in the far north. Here the vegetable broth described as 'hotch-potch' was concocted in 1734. It consisted of turnips ('neeps'), carrots and peas boiled together. Although the *Oxford English Dictionary* defines hotch-potch in cookery as 'a dish containing a mixture of many ingredients', the meaning in Scotland was more specific. To the poorer sections of the community, living mainly on oatmeal—and often little enough of that—the addition of green kale (colewort) and of thick vegetable broth must have been a blessing. The potato came later. First recorded under cultivation at Kirkcudbright in 1725, its potential value as food for the multitude was not fully realised and exploited until the decade 1770-80.

Very different from austere stories by the later 'Kailyard School' is the old romantic tale by Dr John Brown, author of *Rab and His Friends*, who wrote affectionately of the island of Inchmahome, Lake of

Menteith, Perthshire. He describes the place as having 'a loveliness, gentleness and peace about it. . . . You wander through the ruins, overgrown with ferns and Spanish filberts and old fruit trees, and at the corner of the old monkish garden you come upon one of the strangest and most touching sights you ever saw—an oval space of about eighteen feet by twelve, with the remains of a double row of boxwood all round'.

This enclosure is often called 'Queen Mary's Bower', but 'Rab' (as the author became known) prefers to describe it as 'the first garden of her simpleness'. Mary was only five years old when she played there, and not yet able to reign as Queen of Scots. In 1548* she sailed from Dumbarton for France.

The author R. B. Cunninghame Graham, who had some claim to the dormant title of the earldom of Menteith, was buried on Inchmahome in 1936. Moray McLaren gives interesting reasons for the un-Scottish use of 'lake' instead of 'loch' for this piece of water. It may, he thinks, be partly based on its round, rather smooth 'southern' shape, and partly on the fact that it contains coarse fish, including pike, rather than the indigenous Scots trout and salmon.

Less romantic, but possibly even more worth telling, is the story of Edinburgh's Botanic Garden. The traveller, naturalist and physician Andrew Balfour is sometimes called the father of botany in Scotland as well as the father of Scottish gardening. He founded the Botanic Garden in 1670, when, together with his friend Dr Robert Sibbald, first Professor of Medicine at the University of Edinburgh, he began to cultivate medicinal herbs on a plot of land forty feet square in the

* This date is debatable.

policies* of Holyrood. James Sutherland was its first 'intendant'. In Britain only Oxford, with a Physic Garden founded in 1621, takes precedence over the Edinburgh Botanic Garden.

Soon the original piece of land was deemed too small for the enterprise, so in 1676 the founders obtained use of a garden attached to Trinity Hospital—a site now occupied by the east end of Waverley station. Sutherland, hard working and ill paid for his toil, was made King's Botanist and Regius Professor under a royal warrant issued by William III.

In 1761 John Hope, now appointed Regius Keeper (see opposite), transferred the Botanic Garden to a five-acre site on the road to Leith, and managed to obtain from the Crown a permanent income for maintaining it. According to Loudon (see the Reading List, page 73), Dr John Hope first taught the Linnaean system in Scotland. His successor, Daniel Rutherford (uncle to Sir Walter Scott), appears to have taken more interest in chemistry than in plants. Fortunately a fine Scots gardener, William McNab, was persuaded to leave Kew for Edinburgh as principal gardener, and in 1820, under the aegis of Robert Graham, a new Regius Keeper, McNab transferred the contents of the old garden to its present site at Inverleith. This ingenious man invented a machine which enabled him successfully to transplant large trees—a task hitherto regarded as impossible.

A yew tree, planted by James Sutherland in the original plot at Holyrood in 1670, had a long life. In 1763 it was uprooted and replanted on the new site at Leith Walk. In 1882 McNab transplanted this tree, which by now had grown mightily. It survived two moves in its

* Enclosed ground round the mansion-house—from the French *policie*.

6

*Professor John Hope, Regius Keeper, Royal Botanic Garden,
Edinburgh, 1761-86, with one of his gardeners*

first one hundred and fifty years of existence. Everyone who knew the venerable yew hoped that it would reach its third century, but a violent gale in January 1968 blew it right out of the soil, destroying it.

During the yew's lifetime in the present Royal Botanic Garden, the Tropical Palm House was erected, at a cost quoted as 'upwards of £1,500', and the great William McNab's son, James, was installed as his successor, under J. H. Balfour. By 1876 another forty acres of land had been acquired and a large temperate palm house built at a cost of £6,500. In 1889 the garden came wholly under the Crown, controlled by H.M. Office of Works.

With J. H. Balfour's son Isaac Bayley Balfour as Regius Keeper, vast developments were carried out. These included the planting of an arboretum, and the construction of a rock garden and a large range of glasshouses. The laboratories were reorganised and equipment for botanical research and teaching expanded, creating a major centre of research in Edinburgh. Here in 1902 George Forrest, now famous as a plant hunter, began his career in a minor post at the herbarium.

The seven expeditions to Western China and Himalayan regions undertaken by Forrest between 1904 and 1932 provided an enormous amount of work for the scientific staff of the garden, where problems of identification and cultivation of the great mass of new plant material sent home by Forrest were, over some fifty years, successfully researched.

W. Wright Smith, the next Regius Keeper, came to Scotland from the Royal Botanic Herbarium in Calcutta, where he had directed the Botanical Survey of India. He had himself undertaken journeys to Tibet and Himalayan valleys in search of plants, so was well equipped to supervise the studies of Himalayan and Chinese flora being pursued at Edinburgh's Botanic Garden. He also improved the areas of woodland and copse, enlarged the rock garden and constructed the heath and peat gardens.

After his death in 1956 the single combined post of Professor of Botany and Regius Keeper was divided. H. R. Fletcher became Keeper, and Robert Brown Professor of Botany. In 1968 Dr Fletcher was appointed Honorary Professor of Botany at the University of Edinburgh.

From the small collection of medicinal herbs begun in 1670 by Andrew Balfour and Robert Sibbald has grown this splendid collection of plants and trees, which attracts many thousands of ordinary visitors, drawn by its variety and beauty as a garden. At the same time, botanical and horticultural studies carried on behind the scenes are honoured throughout the world by experts in these fields. An account of the garden as it is today will be found later in this book, together with accounts of Glasgow Botanic Garden and other collections of plants which may be described as 'botanic' gardens.

In Scotland the late seventeenth century brought many developments in horticulture and silviculture. Allied to these interests was the issue in 1683 of what was then a work of great novelty—a book on gardening written by a practical gardener. This treatise, *The Scots Gard'ner* by John Reid, was published in Edinburgh and printed by David Lindsay. It is divided into two parts; the first is described as of 'contriving and planting gardens, orchards, avenues, groves, with new and profitable wayes of levelling; and how to measure and divide land'.

The second part covers 'the inspection and improvement of forrest and fruit-trees, kitchen hearbes and fruits, with some physicall [medicinal] hearbes, shrubs and flowers, whereunto is added The Gard'ner's Kalendar published for the climate of Scotland by John Reid, Gard'ner'. In the second edition of this work, dated 1756, the author is described as having been gardener to Sir George Mackenzie of Rosehaugh at Avoch in Ross-shire. The name of Mackenzie has long been associated with fine gardens in that county, notably with Inverewe.

A preface to the original edition, written by the author, is addressed 'to all the ingenious planters of Scotland'. Among his 'weighty reasons' for issuing the book, Reid states that 'many books on gard'nery are for other countries and climates, and many things in them more speculative than practical'. The last reprint, dated 1907, contains an appreciation of Reid by the Earl of Rosebery. My own copy was given to me by the fine Scots poet Andrew Young, who by some strange alchemy became a canon of Chichester Cathedral. He was a keen botanist and garden lover, and an admirer of John Reid.

Reid was essentially practical. How astonishing it would have been for him had anyone been able to foresee the spate of books and articles on practical gardening with which our present libraries are filled—all sprung from the seed he planted. My edition of his treatise measures a mere 6½ inches by 5 inches, and contains 195 pages. In that space Reid managed to include the planning of a house and its surrounding parterres, walks, pavilions, stables, brewhouse and bakehouse, ponds, orchards, kitchen gardens, nurseries and forest trees, as well as directions for planting and maintenance, which in our time often fill several volumes twice as big as Reid's small book.

Unfamiliar today are his instructions about the placing of kitchen gardens near the stables. This is 'for the convenience of wheeling in manure, out of sight of the front of the house: because of the impropriety of the view, to see manure in the garden where the eyes of the persons in the house should be more agreeably entertained'. Now that manure is to most of us a rare prize, few gardeners could wish for more agreeable entertainment than the sight of a good, rich supply being delivered to nourish flowers and vegetables.

In view of the later fashion for oval walled gardens (mentioned in the following chapter), it is a surprise to find Reid urging the landowner to make 'your walls of south aspect in straight lines but not semi-circular, which is by some erroneously practised; for there the wind being pent up occasions squirles, and retards the ripening of the fruit there planted'. Maybe he had not contemplated the plan based on a full circle, or enclosed oval shape.

Even if readers possess no more than a window box, Reid is almost certain to give pleasure to those who scan his pages.

'To lay grass, first level the ground, whether a walke or a plot; and 'tis the better to lye a year so made up, before you lay the turf; because it may be levelled up again, if it sink into holes; if it lye wet, bottom with stones and rubbish; and if the earth be fat, take it out, and put in sand. . . . Let the turf be of equal thickness, near inch and a half thick, a foot and a half broad, and as much in length; lay their green sides together when you put them in the cart, but do not roll them when brought home. Lay them all even and close, feeling each particular turf with your foot, so as you may discern any inequality, to be helped immediately.' Who could read

that without smelling the cut turves—a scent com-
pounded of moist earth (fat or lean) and fresh green
grass—or visualising the careful gardener as he feels
each turf with his foot?

How fond he is of trees and shrubs! 'The black cherrie or geen is a tree I love well in avenues and thickets;
there is a sort at Niddrie-castle, where I was born, seven
miles west from Edinburgh, whose fruit is preferable to
any cherrie.'

His advice on pruning is still valid, although seldom
expressed with such charm today. 'Begin betimes to
prune your fruit-trees; spare them not while young;
reduce them into good shape and order while such, so
they will not only overgrow their wounds, their
branches being but small, but also, when they should
come to bear fruit, you shall not need to cut so much,
only purge them of superfluities; and this is the way to
make trees fruitful as well as pleasant.' A gardener's
version of spare the rod and spoil the child.

Robert Louis Stevenson, in his *Memories and Portraits*, wrote of a garden known to him personally.
Except for the straw hat, his account of the gardener
could as well fit the seventeenth-century John Reid.

'To me . . . he stands essentially as a *genius loci*. It is
impossible to separate his spare form and old straw hat
from the garden in the lap of the hill, with its rocks
overgrown with clematis, its shadowy walks, and the
splendid breadth of champaign that one saw from the
north-west corner. The garden and gardener seem part
and parcel of each other.'

Formal Gardens

IN gardens, as in human affairs, there are degrees of formality. My first choice, Pitmedden, Udny, Aberdeenshire, is so meticulously planned and maintained that it may fairly be said to reach the topmost rung of the ladder. It is situated some fourteen miles north of Aberdeen, and is now a property of the National Trust for Scotland and open to visitors all the year.

This place must have seemed very remote at the time when Sir Alexander Seton of Pitmedden and his wife Dame Margaret Lauder created the 'Great Garden' for the entertainment of their visitors. In 1675 the enclosure in which this pleasance developed—a site of three acres in extent—was overlooked by the Seton's castle, now supplanted by an unfortified mansion-house. It is believed that Sir Alexander found his inspiration at the Palace of Holyroodhouse in Edinburgh, where Charles I had initiated a garden of similar type. That design is shown in 'A Bird's Eye View of Edinburgh', drawn by James Gordon of Rothiemay in 1647.

To those who dwelt in what were then the untutored wastes of heather, whins and mosses of Aberdeenshire, the tightly knit pattern of form and colour within Pitmedden's walls must have seemed an eighth wonder of the world. To the more sophisticated guests of the Setons, the Great Garden may have suggested the latest minuet, danced with precision by a handsome array of well-groomed plants partnered by areas of coloured gravel.

Unfortunately it did not survive for three centuries. The present garden is a reconstruction from the ground up; but one so well made that it has become the finest example of strictly formal gardening to be found in Scotland today. A hundred and fifty years ago, by which time Sir Alexander's splendid project had suffered decline into a mere vegetable patch, who would have thought that its glory could be so cleverly revived for our pleasure in the second half of the twentieth century?

Major James Keith, who presented the property, and The National Trust for Scotland, which sponsored restoration of the original garden, deservedly share the gratitude of all garden-lovers who are able to visit Pitmedden. The estate passed from the Setons to the Keiths in 1894, and Major James Keith, the last laird, was a practical farmer who improved his lands with vision and enterprise which earned him a leading place among Scottish agriculturists. He gave Pitmedden to the Trust in 1952, with an endowment for its upkeep, and almost at once plans were set on foot to re-create Sir Alexander Seton's garden.

The inherent difficulty of the project was increased because no plan of the original layout could be found. In 1818 a fire which destroyed Seton family portraits and papers, had in all likelihood been responsible also for the loss of garden designs. The late Dr James Richardson, who prepared the modern scheme, based three of the four sections of the parterre on those depicted by James Gordon at Holyroodhouse, and contrived the fourth as a tribute to Sir Alexander Seton.

To quote from a description by R. J. Prentice, 'The principal feature, set in a parallelogram flanked by representations of the Scottish saltire and thistle, is his coat-of-arms. In the first and fourth quarters there are the three crescents of the Setons and, in the centre of these, a man's heart with drops of blood issuing from it

14

to commemorate the death of John Seton in the service of King Charles I. The motto *Sustento Sanguine Signa*, "I bear the standard with blood", also refers to the slaying of Sir Alexander's father at the Brig o' Dee. The second motto, *Merces Haec Certa Laborum*, "This is the sure reward of our labours", is shown at the lower edge of the composition.

'The crest is omitted, but it is exhibited in the form of weather vanes set over the pavilion roofs. These show demi-figures of a soldier in late seventeenth-century uniform holding the banner of Scotland. A facsimile of the Royal Standard carried by Sir Alexander now flies from one flagpole in the upper garden, and the saltire or St Andrew's Cross from another.'

The elaborate heraldic pattern of this Seton parterre—the north-west section of the whole design—carries the initials SAS for Sir Alexander Seton and DML for Dame Margaret Lauder, his wife. The south-east parterre, with its legend *Tempus Fugit*, has as centrepiece an intricately fashioned sundial of the same date as the original Great Garden. Between 1860 and 1958 it stood on the north side of Pitmedden House. So far as is known, only one other of this type exists. The globe-shaped sundial with twenty-four facets is able to use the sun at all times of year. It is far more complicated than the flat single-gnomon dial commonly found in old English gardens.

George Barron, the head gardener responsible for planting this unique restoration, told me that to outline the patterns called for six miles of box edging. He said it was all trimmed with hand-shears, "making a far better job". At the time of my visit a few years ago the designs were filled in with no fewer than 30,000 annual plants, each one pricked out by the patiently devoted Mrs Barron. After the land had been cleared and levelled,

15

creation of the pattern began in 1956, and the first 'colour'—apart from tinted stones—was planted to fulfil the plan by 1958.

What excitement for those who carried out this ambitious scheme, when for the first season it came alive on the ground! There are many difficulties to be overcome in getting plants of the requisite colours to bloom at the same time, particularly in the changeable weather conditions of this north-eastern part of Britain, not far from the sea coast. Experience has gradually shown which bedders best fulfil the task, and when I last saw the parterre in early September it looked fine, although Mr Barron thought I should have come a little earlier. This is standard practice on the part of most gardeners, as Ruth Draper so well displayed in her act 'Showing the garden'. "If only you had come last week. . . ."

The brilliant colours and consistent performance of present-day annuals are admirably suited to highly formal arrangements, however incongruous here in the strictly historical sense. Some purists may object that Sir Alexander Seton's original garden could not have been stuffed with begonias and alyssum; but would not seventeenth-century gardeners have welcomed the wide choice available today? To my mind, modern 'bedders' are used to the greatest advantage at Pitmedden.

Stiff and solid as many of them are, seldom looking their best when spotted about in the little 'mixed' gardens which most of us own, they are in their element in massed array. Edged by rigidly clipped box, they resemble a mosaic of stained glass or enamel, fitted into firmly defined shapes. Coming within the walls from the somewhat austere landscape of Aberdeenshire— once described as 'the great cold shoulder of Scotland'—the visitor, as he looks down from the ter-

16

race, feels grateful for the patches of strong heraldic colour and not at all disposed to call them garish.

Smooth areas of grass are there, too, to set off the design, and a wide walk containing a double row of clipped yews, ten a side, which seem like twenty identical twins (see over). These have an interesting history. George Barron went over to France to study the art of topiary expressly for the work of remaking this Pitmedden garden. On his return he fashioned light wooden frames of lattice-work—corsets for his yews—and for some time the little plants were sheared close to the frames. Here was another kind of strict training for young growths which John Reid would surely have approved (see page 12). Mr Barron also studied the art of pleaching (the intertwining of branches), and a fine avenue of pleached limes has resulted.

Against the terrace wall there are huge buttresses of yew, shaped like the arms of club chairs, which form sheltered alcoves to house roses, clematis and honeysuckle. Two immense herbaceous borders, designed by Lady Burnett of Leys (creator of the plantings at Crathes) are boldly filled with traditional favourites, such as monkshood of a dark purplish-blue which looks well with red-hot poker, campanula, golden rod, and white plumes of spiraea. These all grow up through lengths of six-inch mesh nylon netting, stretched above the borders when the plants are about a foot high. Firm support is essential for such tall, soft top-hamper when fierce gales come straight off the North Sea.

On the wall opposite the terrace are fan-trained plums and espalier apples—Beauty of Bath, Worcester Pearmain, Peasgood's Nonsuch and others—echoing in their geometrical, precise order the accurate patterns of the parterre. When I came upon this wall, with ripe, perfect apples hanging at regular intervals like gold and

Pitmedden, North East Parterre

18

red lights on a Christmas tree, I was instantly taken back to days spent poring over nursery books, with coloured pictures of the Kate Greenaway period.

There is much else to delight the visitor. Of the two gazebos or pavilions, elegant little buildings with ogee-shaped roofs, which are placed at either end of the top terrace, the north is approximately in its original state, the other carefully restored. Cheerful sounds made by running water come from a central fountain supplied by an old conduit unearthed by Dr Richardson. This fountain has been given a paved surround made of pebbles taken out of the River Dee. They were split with a hammer and laid, flat side up, in patterns—a revival of a very old craft, perfectly suited to the mood of Pitmedden, where it is difficult to find a jarring note.

A garden of similar period may be visited at Edzell in the neighbouring county of Angus. The ruined castle, now an Ancient Monument, was originally the seat of the Stirlings. It passed to the Lindsays of Glenesk, and in the sixteenth century the 9th Earl of Crawford added a quadrangular mansion-house. Completed in 1602 by his son Sir David Lindsay, Lord Edzell, this edifice was then given a pleasance or *viridarium*, which has considerable charm and is beautifully maintained. Like Pitmedden, it is a reconstruction.

When it was first made, the garden lay within the confines of a moat, a defence swept away by floodwaters in the eighteenth century. It formed a strait-jacket for Sir David's project, which is consequently only about one-sixth the size of Pitmedden's Great Garden. In fact, the difference in size leaves the visitor with cause to remember the adjective 'Great' for Sir Alexander Seton's enterprise.

Apart from comparisons of scale, I find Edzell less

satisfying than Pitmedden. Possibly the intricate decoration of the wall, including sculptured panels derived from the work of a German artist, detracts from the floral excellence of the parterre—they do not so much complement one another as compete for attention, and by so doing reduce the visual attraction of the whole. That 'certain modesty', which R. J. Prentice mentions as governing the Seton conception, seems more successful in blending the sum of its parts into one harmonious whole.

The Royal Palace of Falkland in Fife sounds a likely place at which to come upon a formal garden of early date, but the visitor who looks for knots or parterres will be disappointed. From the fifteenth century the Stuarts were interested in garden care, and accounts showing wages paid in 1456 to gardeners have survived; yet of their gardening all trace has gone. By the end of the Second World War this ground was producing little but potatoes.

Fortunately the old real tennis court escaped being dug over for food production. It is the only example in Scotland and resembles the court built by the uncle of James V—Henry VIII—at his palace of Hampton Court beside the Thames. In real tennis the ball is struck with the hand. Racquets were not in use when these courts were made. A fringed or tasselled rope divided the court, as a net does in the modern game. It is said that real tennis is the oldest and most difficult of all ball games.

Records show that a great lawn existed five centuries ago, where Queen Mary of Gilderland walked. The present sward extends also to the loaning beneath the castle, where her grandson, James V, practised archery at the long butts. These mementoes of Stuart games and sports survive, but of their pleasance there is nothing left.

The floral display is a twentieth-century design by Percy Cane, and consists mainly of a gigantic mixed border and six large island beds. Rambling in profusion over the walls are clematis, roses and an outsize Russian Vine. The redevelopment of this flower garden was begun in 1947 by the Hereditary Keeper, Major Michael Crichton Stuart. When it had become established, he appointed The National Trust for Scotland his Deputy Keeper, thus ensuring its continuance and the safety of Palace and garden for all time. Although a modern garden, Percy Cane's layout seems to complement the Palace with complete success. Given a warm summer day, it is a lovely place to linger in.

A different kind of formality is found in the so-called 'Italian' garden. I have chosen one on the grand scale at Drummond Castle in Perthshire, and another, smaller, simpler, and delicately wrought, at The Lennel in Berwickshire, near Coldstream and the Border.

Drummond Castle, seat of the Earl of Ancaster, was founded in 1491 by John, Lord Drummond, whose descendants became Earls of Perth. It is situated two miles south of Crieff on the Muthill road, and approached by an avenue a mile long. The garden, laid out on a series of natural rock terraces, is an example of formality on so ambitious a scale that it is difficult at first sight not to feel intimidated by such overwhelming grandeur.

William Robinson (1838-1935), friend of Gertrude Jekyll and pioneer of the 'natural' garden, was not easily impressed. He wrote a scathing attack on this garden, calling it a display of bedding in its cruder forms— 'plants in squares, repeated by hundreds and thousands, and walks from which all interest is taken by the planting on each side being of exactly the same pattern'. Robinson called it 'the deplorable result of trying to adapt Italian modes to English gardens'. If we are able to disregard prejudices and accept many styles for the variety they give to the garden scene, it must be said that this grandiose conception fits the slopes and subtle changes of level, and accords well with the great house, of which a tower is the sole relic of the original fortress.

When I saw it, there was very little showy bedding-out. The colour was light in key, with a great deal of white and silver, like ribbons binding all those walks of mown grass, clipped shrubs, statues, fountains, sundials and box edging. Anaphalis ('Pearl Flower') and the fragrant 'Curry Plant' (*Helichrysum angustifolium* or *H. siculum*) furnished most of the silver borders. The bank immediately below the mansion was divided into a kind of irregular jigsaw pattern, in subdued but richer colours, composed chiefly of heaths, brooms, hypericums and potentillas.

It seems impossible to get a satisfactory picture of this garden, perhaps because the only viewpoint from which to assimilate the whole would be from the building, into which visitors are not allowed to go. Few landowners in Britain are still able to keep up such a huge place. For this reason alone it should be seen once in a lifetime. Also, it is far better kept than most gardens I have seen in Italy.

If you could dash straight from Drummond Castle to Lennel, and spend an hour or two in each garden during visiting times on the same day, the contrast would be pointed. Where the first seeks above all to impress, Lennel is surely designed to soothe and enrich the spirit of the beholder. The overwhelming sense of the amount of work involved in the care of Drummond is entirely absent from Lennel. It is tended with equal diligence and skill, but no feeling of strain emerges. Perhaps the River Tweed flowing steadily at the foot of the garden produces a therapeutic effect. Even on the wildest March day, Mother Tweed seems undisturbed.

Lennel, with its dignified Georgian house, belongs to Sir Ilay Campbell. Smooth grassed walks arranged on a series of narrow terraces parallel with the river; long rectangular pools filled with water-lilies, at the lowest level; some venerable trees; a profusion of roses, lilies, hollyhocks, delphiniums, astrantias and other familiar delights—all combine with splendid old walls, steps, sculptures and gate pillars of Berwickshire stone, to form what might be termed an 'English' style of Italian garden, situated inside the borders of Scotland. If critical analysis fails to attract attention, people should stroll in and enjoy themselves without worrying about styles of gardening. The Lennel makes it easy.

Some gardens create mirth. Without disrespect, I consider the garden at Earlshall in Fife to be highly entertaining. The whole is no more than two acres in size, and about a quarter of that holds the joke— thirty-two (or is it slightly more?) clipped yews, shaped like chessmen. Here they stand, bishops and knights, kings and queens, castles and pawns, not solemnly spaced out on a chequer board, but closely congregated like people at a cocktail party. By certain effects of light, when the sun is low, you can vow that heads wag together on stiff necks of yew wood. Some topiary pepper-pots, peacocks and buttresses of yew complete the assembly.

A stout holly hedge, such as John Evelyn, the diarist, delighted in, divides the chessmen from a vegetable garden. In spite of its shelter, the south-westerly gales cause enough turbulence to make any head shake. Although the clipped yews appear to have been established here for centuries, they are putting on an act to deceive the stranger. The grey stone walls and crow-stepped gables of the castle have stood for over four hundred years; but the yews are what Scots call 'incomers'. They were transplanted in 1895 from a derelict Edinburgh garden by Sir Robert Lorimer, who completed his restoration of the place at the beginning of this century. The sandy soil of Fife is appreciated by yews, so notwithstanding their seniority they survived the move and flourish here.

They are companioned by 'old' roses; some interesting shrubs and trees, such as Californian Mock Orange (*Carpenteria*) and the autumn flame-tree, *Parrotia persica*; the shrubby Starwort (*Microglossa albescens*), and many herbaceous plants. Lorimer was fond of pebble paving, which has been used in random patterns. Over the garden door is a quotation from *As You Like It*: 'HERE SHALL YE SEE NO ENEMY BUT WINTER AND ROUGH WEATHER'.

Mr and Mrs Arthur Purvis bought Earlshall in 1926. During their absence in the Second World War, a housekeeper stayed in charge, firmly insisting that she had no fear although alone in the castle. It was so impregnable, she thought, that neither bombs from above nor invaders on the ground could harm the occupant—and none did.

It seems appropriate to include among formal designs that curious and rare phenomenon, the oval walled garden. Whether the plantings of today are symmetrical patterns or not, the curved boundary walls bestow some

24

degree of formality, and must have been conceived as enclosures for parterres.

The example at Netherbyres near the fishing port of Eyemouth on the coast of Berwickshire belongs now to the Furness family, and has been skilfully maintained for many years by Flower, Lady Furness—herself very much a down-to-earth gardener.

Probably designed by a former owner, William Crow, who was of a mathematical and mechanical turn of mind (and who died of the palsy in 1750), the garden is enclosed by an elliptical wall. It is a double wall, the outer side constructed of local stone, the inner lined with Dutch bricks, brought by sea to Eyemouth—then a thriving seaport with a big export trade in wool and linen.

The enclosure measures about two hundred yards by one hundred, and was for long sheltered by belts of trees, which road-widening in recent years has depleted. An elegant glass-house dates from the second half of the nineteenth century. Fruit trees trained against the brick walls obtained the maximum amount of light and air owing to the curved construction—the ripening of fruit was the main object of the exercise it appears. Part of the present floral display is arranged within formal shapes of clipped box (see over).

Berwickshire can boast of two oval walled gardens, possibly copied one from the other and assisted by the availability of imported bricks. The second is situated at Carolside, a mile to the north of Earlston. Far below the A68 road to Lauder, the Adam-style house of Sir John and Lady Mary Gilmour may be seen in its setting of broad green valley where the Leader Water runs.

Lady Mary is a lover of 'old' roses and has made here the best collection in the Borders. This is almost a 'cottage' garden in style, casual and unpretentious.

Oval Walled Garden, Netherbyres

Fruit trees act host to *Rosa filipes*, Paul's Himalayan musk rose has thrust its pink rosettes to the top of a large willow, and on the ground are fragrant herbs—marjoram, thyme, curry plant and the bush artemisia, Southernwood, which Scots call Apple Ringie, above the gold flower-foam of Lady's Mantle.

Two ancient thorn bushes on a knoll near the front door have a history worth telling. In 1790 Lady Sarah Lennox (Bunbury) eloped with Lord William Adam Gordon and took refuge here at Carolside. To commemorate their happiness they planted the thorns, one each. Before long the Duke of Richmond, scandalised by his sister's behaviour, forced her to return with him to Goodwood. Only the thorn bushes were left together. In human affairs, formality triumphed.

Opening hours at Pitmedden and Falkland are arranged by the National Trust for Scotland. The rest of the gardens here named will be found in the booklet *Scotland's Gardens*.

'Natural' Gardens

THE most natural-looking gardens are those consisting wholly or largely of woodland, with shade-loving shrubs and plants beneath the trees, and drifts of sun-lovers in open glades. Gertrude Jekyll had a masterly touch with this sort of arrangement. The garden of Inverewe on the west coast of Ross-shire was never visited by Miss Jekyll, but undoubtedly she would have approved of its wayward informality. Yet in truth few gardens are less natural than this one. It is a dream—one man's dream, maintained after his death by his daughter, and all done with amazing artistry and skill by the pair of them. Not for nothing has it been called 'The Miracle of Inverewe'.

In 1852 Osgood Hanbury Mackenzie, scion of an ancient and green-fingered West Highland family, acquired a bleak, bare promontory overlooking Loch Ewe and set about planning a garden there. In later years he put the story into a book, which is still in print.*

'In the year 1862,' he wrote, 'my mother bought for me the two adjoining estates of Inverewe and Kernsary on the west coast of Ross-shire . . . and after taking two years to settle where we should make our home, we finally pitched upon the neck of a barren peninsula as the site of the house. I had all my life [he was only twenty] longed to begin gardening and planting . . . so my mother undertook the whole trouble of house-building and I set myself to the rest of the work.'

Fifty years later, in 1914, the turreted Victorian man-

* *A Hundred Years in the Highlands* (Bles).

28

sion built by the mother was burnt out, while her son's garden still flourishes and has become world-famous. The present house of Inverewe, modelled on South African examples admired by Osgood's daughter, the late Mairi Sawyer, was built in 1937 after her second marriage. During the interim period, the Mackenzies lived in the white lodge at the gates of Inverewe, enlarged after the fire to house the family.

Most accounts issued today state that no trees grew on the promontory except one dwarf willow. The picture-map sold to visitors in Mrs Sawyer's day says there were two. In any case it, or they, were insignificant midgets. Osgood Mackenzie began to plant trees here in 1864, knowing that thick shelter-belts were essential to protect his garden. Screens of Scots pine of good old stock (like some still seen on the shores of Loch Maree) were mixed with Corsican pine, rowan, larch, beech, Douglas fir, and laced with hedges of the native *Rhododendron ponticum*.

The peninsula could boast of little good soil, hardly any gravel or sand, but it did have veins of a soft pink clay, amid a jumble of rocks which in places broke up easily. Certain trees, notably the Wellingtonia (so recently introduced into Britain, and very fashionable), were treated to pockets of imported soil. An old man carried it up on his back in wickerwork creels. Labour was plentiful and extremely cheap in those days,* and the people worked long hours without complaint.

Am Ploc Ard, meaning 'The High Lump', is the Gaelic name for the Inverewe promontory. Although it is only about one hundred feet above sea-level, Osgood soon found that it caught all the gales that blew, most of them salt-laden. The heavy rainfall averaged sixty inches a year. On the credit side, snow seldom lay, hard

* The men who made a road up to the Fionn Loch earned a shilling a day.

frosts were rare at that time, and the temperature of sea and land was raised by the Gulf Stream.

For their first five years in this exposure the shelter-belts 'grew down instead of up', as the Mackenzies put it. The young trees were endeavouring to anchor themselves by good roots, although some were forced to spread out like shallow plates above shelves of impenetrable rock. I saw these root-formations myself, when in the gale of December 1952 a hundred and fifty of Osgood Mackenzie's trees came crashing down the brae beside Inverewe House. Next morning I took some horrifying pictures of the scene, marvelling that for seventy years these tall trees had managed to stand on such shallow roots. Gales there must always have been; but this one came from the north—a most unusual quarter—and cut a swathe from top to bottom of the High Lump. In general, the climate had been considerably milder in her father's youth, Mrs Sawyer said.

She also mentioned that in the nineteenth century game was far more plentiful on the estate, and yet the young trees had fewer destructive enemies than in her time. Grouse were abundant, but caused no harm. Black game picked out the leading buds of Scots pine, which only served to make them grow bushy. Brown and blue hares removed some shoots from Austrian pine and oak; but on the whole, trees and game coexisted fairly well. The rabbit plague had not yet begun, and there were fewer roe deer—those stealthy and determined robbers whose depredations Mrs Sawyer feared and detested.

Her father, that astonishing young man, waited another fifteen years before his game-pruned shelter grew thick enough for the planting of more tender subjects to begin. To try these out, he cleared small spaces of heather and crowberry and fenced them

30

against deer. Eucalyptus and Tree Fern, never before introduced so far north in Britain—roughly the same latitude as Goose Bay—were put in and seemed to thrive. Encouraged, he went on to plant Arbutus, Griselinia, Cordyline, Phormium and Bamboo. (This book is not designed to hold many Latin names, so those who want a comprehensive plant list must consult the Inverewe guide issued by The National Trust for Scotland. The last time I counted there were 500 named, without the collection of rhododendrons.)

On an old sea beach Osgood Mackenzie had a large walled garden made, this being the only level strip of land that was free from rock. Its soil was a mixture of three parts pebble to one part good black earth. As each man dug his section he had a girl or boy alongside him to gather and remove the stones—a back-breaking sort of task which children of crofters in Wester Ross were still doing in the 1950s. Fresh soil was brought to the new garden from the bed of the loch and from old turf dykes elsewhere on the estate. Above the beach level a second terrace was carved from the hillside, and a great retaining wall built against the rock. Above this runs the present drive entrance to the Inverewe policies.

Osgood in his book writes amusingly of his walled enclosure—'the "kitchen garden", as my English friends take care to call it. As is often the case with us in the Highlands, I possess only the one garden for fruit, flowers and vegetables. It was mostly made out of an old sea-beach, and even now, in spite of a wall and a good sea-bank, the Atlantic threatens occasionally to walk in at its lower doors, and the Great Northern Divers, who float about lazily just outside, appear quite fascinated by the brilliant colours inside when the lower doors are left open for their benefit'.

Before his shelter-belts were fully grown Osgood

married, and in 1878 his only child, Mairi, was born. She, too, had green fingers and planted her first rhododendrons at the age of ten. For this experiment she chose a tiny island in a lochan opposite the house of Tournaig, a mile or two from the Inverewe gates. At the time that house also belonged to the Mackenzies.

Soon Mairi became her father's inseparable companion and fellow-gardener, a partnership in no way lessened by her marriage to a Hanbury cousin in 1907. Their two children did not survive. Osgood Mackenzie died in 1922 and Robert Hanbury eleven years later. In 1935 his widow married Captain Ronald Sawyer, and soon the couple started to plan the rebuilding of Inverewe House. Neither of Mairi's husbands knew much about gardening, but they helped to run the estate and gave her horticultural work every encouragement. Like her father, she was a Gaelic speaker and spoke in that tongue to her employees.

Scotland, even more than England, has regarded horticulture very much as a man's world, and sometimes it seems that insufficient credit is given to Mrs Sawyer for her knowledge and skill in maintaining and developing her father's garden. From its inception in 1864 to her sudden and untimely death in 1953, a period of ninety years, Osgood was in sole charge for the first thirty years; Mairi became an active partner of his for the next three decades; and for the last three she managed it alone. In all, she had sixty years' experience, which equalled that of her more famous father.

How proud he was of the garden they both loved so well, and of his devoted daughter, to whom his book is dedicated. It was a 'proud and happy day' when, in the latter part of Edward VII's reign, he showed his mature garden to 'Mr Bean of Kew'—presumably W. J. Bean, whose books on trees are still in demand. 'I had the pleasure of showing him my Tricuspidarias [Crinoden-drons], Embothriums and Eucryphias, my palms, loquats, Drimys, giant Olearias, Metrosideros and Mit-rarias, etc. . . . Some of the less common varieties are a nice specimen of *Podocarpus totara*, from which Maoris used to make their war canoes, and *Dicksonia antarctica* [Tree Fern], raised from spores ripened in Arran.' He goes on and on, but those Latin names are not for this brief study.

Since 1952, when the garden at Inverewe became a property of The National Trust for Scotland (by gift of Mairi Sawyer), it has gradually become known as a 'rhododendron garden', something we did not hear in her lifetime. Certainly there is a collection of mag-nificent specimens—still largely her own favourites, the natural species—and she grew them to perfection, without crowding; but it is unlikely that she would have cared for the limited scope of such a title.

In his book her father made only one reference to rhododendrons, among other 'strangers which seed freely'. Mairi Sawyer, adding to the latest edition, briefly listed some of 'wild species which seed freely', and named three which survived the unusually severe winter of 1946-7. Inverewe contains a very wide range of plants, catering for many specialist interests as well as for the simple love of gardens. I can recall an incident of the 1950s to show this. Somebody in charge of a visiting party telephoned to inquire how long it would take to go round the garden, which is a little more than fifty acres in extent. Mairi Sawyer gave this reply: "At least an hour for ordinary tourists, two to three hours for garden lovers, and anything up to a week for botanists."

Afterwards I added that for the artist and lover of pictures, a whole lifetime would not be too much. This was surely the greatest achievement of Osgood

Mackenzie and his daughter. They created a garden of disarmingly natural appearance, in which exotic immigrants from as far apart as Chile and New Zealand, Sikkim and Australia had been fitted together to form a perfectly harmonious whole (see opposite).

How much of their skill and taste was innate and spontaneous, and how much the result of careful contrivance, will never be known. Now and then Mrs Sawyer let fall some opinion which suggested that her apparently artless ways owed more to her modest desire not to pontificate than to any lack of thought.

On one occasion she complained to me that English friends pressed her to plant some large herbaceous borders. "Why should I be expected to have those masses of colour here? I hate them. They belong to the south and would look all wrong in this garden. Anyhow, we usually get gales in July, just when that top-heavy growth is tallest. It would be slashed to pieces overnight."

As a sop to such friends she grudgingly made room for a thin line of herbaceous plants between lawn and drive in front of the house. This caused some bewilderment to those who cared for the garden after her death. Why had this great gardener been content with such a poor apology for a herbaceous border? Strenuous efforts were made to remedy the defect. But Mairi had been right, of course. It never really looked at home, and a few years later a report from Inverewe mentioned dishevelment caused by a July gale of winter severity, which broke off spikes of the tallest delphiniums when these were at their best.*

It is inevitable that strangers should take time to understand the complex character of Inverewe, and the Trust is faced with demands that were unknown to the

* Report dated February 1957 refers to summer of 1956.

Chusan Palm and Tree Fern, Inverewe

Mackenzies. Because what is commonly known as 'colour' (i.e., flowers in masses) is thought to be essential in July and August, the peak holiday time for tourists, there is temptation to fill up beds with the more usual sorts of herbaceous or even bedding plants. Were she alive today, I can well suppose that the cool, sensible voice of Mairi Sawyer would be heard to ask why people who wanted these displays could not turn their attention to gardens farther south, which in July and August put on a tremendous show. To those who enjoy subtleties of foliage and form, Inverewe is a delight at all seasons, including winter.

The fashion for 'natural' woodland gardens, begun in Scotland by Osgood Mackenzie, spread rapidly down the west coast from Wester Ross to Galloway. Each garden has its own individual charm—no two are alike, so the tourist who was heard to remark that if you saw one you had seen all of them was clearly in too much of a hurry to be discriminating.

Since 1958 The National Trust for Scotland has owned the splendours of Brodick Castle on the Isle of Arran, which has a fine woodland garden wherein the late Duchess of Montrose built up one of the best collections of rhododendrons in Britain, and a formal garden 250 years old under whose walls tender plants thrive in the open. Some came from the Edinburgh Botanic Garden, many more from Tresco Abbey in the Isles of Scilly—as far to the south-west as one can go in the United Kingdom. Since the death of Sir James Horlick, a collection of hybrid rhododendrons raised by him at Achamore (Gigha) is being transferred to Brodick.

A little farther down Scotland's west coast, still within sight of Arran's hills, are the huge castle and grounds of Culzean*—also run by the Trust. This has something for everybody. The Georgian magnificence of Robert Adam's castle (open to the public) presides over terraces, orangery, herbaceous borders, fountain court, cabbage palms, walled garden, woodland walks and a 'country park' with exhibition centre. Like Inverewe and Brodick, it has superb vistas of sea and peaks.

In private hands are the late Colonel Sir James Horlick's fascinating island garden on Gigha (by Tayinloan); Sir Ilay Campbell's Crarae by Inveraray—a lovely Argyllshire glen full of interesting trees and shrubs, with old-established rhododendrons; and Glenarn, Rhu, Dunbartonshire, a collector's paradise which really qualifies for a place in the chapter on botanic gardens. These are open at frequent intervals in summer. Many other west-coast gardens, open occasionally, are listed in the booklet *Scotland's Gardens*.

A garden on the opposite sea-coast of Scotland—at Tyninghame, near Dunbar—belongs to the Earl and Countess of Haddington. It is a glorious mixture of woodland, rose garden, herbaceous border, parterre of formal excellence (made in 1828), shrubberies and specimen trees, a splendid espaliered apple-walk some 115 yards long (see over), and a four-acre walled garden which contains some of the best yew hedges in Scotland. It should be a happy choice for visits, because East Lothian has a low rainfall (about twenty-four inches a year) and a high sunshine record. Even so, the gardener has troubles. Lady Haddington wrote: 'Traditionally East Lothian is recognised as the "Garden of Scotland" because of its temperate climate, but in spring the east wind can leave a trail of havoc.'

* Pronounced 'Cullane'.

Apple Walk, Tyninghame

Rose Garden, Tyninghame

39

Lady Haddington has a skilful way with roses. Not only has she made a fine rose-garden with an acre of 'old' roses in great variety, but she has been remarkably successful in arranging modern roses to harmonise with the old mansion and its surroundings (see previous page). She avoids the harsher, orange-red hues and confines her plantings to the lighter pinks and pale yellows and white, set off by shrubs such as Notcutt's *Cotinus coggyria*, whose wine-dark foliage gives depth to the design, with silver ground-cover to add sparkle.

In a grassy hollow at the heart of this immense but restful garden lies its greatest treasure—the remains of a little Norman church, St Baldred's, a relic of the long-departed monks of Tyninghame. The church is approached through an avenue of lime-trees and in summer is embalmed in the scent of limes, fragrances of rose and herb and that pungent Australian member of the Myrtle family, Eucalyptus, in which the Earl of Haddington takes a particular interest. His forebears won great renown in Scotland for their forestry. Many grand specimens of trees on this estate date from 1707, the year of Union with England.

One of Scotland's most famous gardeners, William McNab, who went to the Edinburgh Botanic Garden from Kew in 1810, served his apprenticeship at Tyninghame. In 1870 another well-known man, William Brotherston, who wrote *Gardening in the North*, became head gardener here, and after long service was succeeded by his son. R. P. Brotherston wrote *The Book of Cut Flowers*, published in 1906. This was the very first book devoted solely to the modern art of flower-arranging. No doubt Lady Haddington will also go down in the annals of Tyninghame as a brilliant maker and restorer of gardens.

Another home of the Baillie-Hamiltons—Mellerstain

near Kelso—owes much of its charm to her unerring taste. It is occupied by the Earl's heir, Lord Binning. From the south front there is a remarkable vista of green lawn descending to a lake by way of Lady Haddington's rose-planted terraces, with the great humps of the Cheviots beyond. The distance separating house from lake has been made to appear longer than it is by means of a device known as 'false perspective'. The boundary hedges are set on converging rather than parallel lines. The illustration (see over) shows this from the wrong end, to make clear how it is done.

The same picture, taken in conjunction with that of a planting on the seaward edge of the Inverewe policies (see page 43), demonstrates the value of selecting the right plant for the scene. The wild, remote charms of Inverewe need the slenderest small-cupped narcissi; while Mellerstain's Adam elegance is suited to a refined variety of trumpet 'daffodil'. It is slightly heavier in build and more showy than those beside Loch Ewe, although far removed from the chunky modern 'King Alfred' and his like, which look good in cities.

Some gardens do not fit into the formal category, yet have little room to develop a natural effect. They are in-betweens, but none the worse for that.

On Scotland's northern coast, east of Dunnet Head and facing across the Pentland Firth to the looming cliffs of Orkney and the Old Man of Hoy, is the Castle of Mey. The Queen Mother graciously gave access to the castle as well as the garden, so after doing justice to a feast of home-baking made by the housekeeper, Mrs Webster, I went up a stone stair and saw, from a window of the royal study, an attractive vista of woodland at the end of a path between roses and lilies.

"Ah yes," said Mr Sinclair, who presides over the

Mellerstain in spring

Spring flowers at Inverewe

gardens. "The Queen Mother goes out and plants things in that little wood herself." Like his father before him he has worked here all his life, the last twenty years in the service of the present owner. Doubtless his store of calm unshakeable confidence is appreciated by her. He showed me a white sidalcea, something a friend had given the Queen Mother, who herself planted it near the front of a border inside the walled garden. "Too high for the position, of course—far too high," he said; then added indulgently, "But you have to give and take, you know." If he had a theme song, it might have been 'Queens may come and queens may go, but gardens and gardeners endure forever'.

Whatever its past history, this is now a peaceful and home-like castle. In the entrance lobby younger members of the royal family had made a sea-garden with weed and shells. Within a two-acre walled garden were sweetpeas, primulas and lilies (*L. henreyii*) cheek-by-jowl with fruit and vegetables. Mr Sinclair said the Queen Mother has a liking for herbs, and her chef knows how to use them, so he provides a handsome collection of tarragon, fennel, chives, rue, dill, hyssop, lemon balm, sage, thyme and parsley. All are overhung by rose Albertine, which scrambles on the walls, and fragrant bushes of Apple Ringie.

Opposite the walled garden is a curious fence made of stone slabs set up on end, like tombstones. I have only once before seen such construction, and that was in the Cotswold village of Filkins, near Lechlade. Now that I think about it, the Queen Mother's little weather-beaten wood is more of a novelty in Caithness than anything made of stone.

A long way farther south—in Nairnshire, not far from Inverness—the great castle of Cawdor, seat of the Earl of that name, is open to visitors in summer months.

Its grandeur looms above a walled flower garden which has by contrast a rather touching air of simplicity. Here is an old, loved, used garden—very much a family affair, not made into a show place. Coming to a walk planted with the tawny *Lilium henreyii* and white *Galtonia candicans*, I was greeted by a flock of white fantail pigeons, who pitched close to my feet and strutted up the path ahead of me.

A pair of lichened sumach trees looked as old as the hills. Some equally ancient pears and apples placidly nursed roses and clematis in their boughs. A small box-edged parterre accompanied topiary shapes, Tweedledum and Tweedledee, and a wistaria trained like a corkscrew. Silver plants had spread lavishly—artemisias, cinerarias and *Hebe pagei*, to name a few—with quantities of lavender near the castle.

Lower down the garden, clipped Irish yews ran true to form. Here, as in the garden of Chiefswood near Melrose (given by Sir Walter Scott to his daughter Sophia), the dark green variety stand up stiffly straight, while the gold sort adopt sinuous curves, like candles beginning to melt in the sun.

Underneath a venerable common yew, which leans aslant a grassy patch, children—now vanished—had laid out a doll's tea-party. The pigeons, their pink eyes rounder than ever, snatched up crumbs without a please or thank you.

In the separate vegetable garden the head gardener, Mr Wood, showed the remains of a huge wild cat—thirty-eight inches from nose to tail—recently shot on the estate. Being greatly troubled by birds, he had stuffed the skin and suspended the fearsome creature from a fishing swivel above his greenstuff. "It keeps the pigeons away," he said, "but the blackbirds are too canny to mind it."

Perhaps the most famous castle garden in the north is Crathes on Deeside, some fourteen miles west of Aberdeen. An ancient home of the Burnetts of Leys, it was handed over to The National Trust for Scotland in 1951. An old lime avenue, a 'toad-stool' of clipped Portugal laurel and some great yew hedges were all planted in the early years of the eighteenth century. They are beautifully maintained today—it takes two men six weeks to clip the yews—and play an important part in a garden which, like that of Falkland Palace, is a twentieth-century creation.

At Crathes no professional landscape gardener was engaged. The late Sir James and Lady Burnett designed and planted it together, he a connoisseur of shrubs and trees, she with a love of herbaceous plants and a flair for arrangement. On the six acres of enclosed ground near the castle, this husband-and-wife team built up what is now one of Scotland's most visited gardens.

It is sometimes described as a 'room' garden and compared with Hidcote and Sissinghurst, both of which I know well. To my mind the analogy is rather forced. The internal divisions at Crathes are open, not secretive, and do not induce a feeling of discovery as the stranger progresses from one to another. The basic character of Crathes is more natural than formal, and the brilliant medley of the 'June' border, together with Sir James's collection of shrubs and trees, are the most satisfactory parts of the garden, seen as adjuncts to the upstanding bulk of the cream-harled building. The experiments with 'blue' and 'gold' gardens and a 'white' border are a little too suggestive of Victorian drawing-rooms to suit this place, although they are certainly very pretty in themselves.

Crathes Castle is open in summer, its garden all the year. The Castle of Cawdor and its gardens are open in

46

summer. The Castle of Mey is open a few times during the peak holiday season. Mention of all three properties will be found in the booklet *Scotland's Gardens*, which also gives full details of Dawyck.

Three families who have been associated with the estate of Dawyck in Peeblesshire—the Veitches, from the middle of the fifteenth century; the Naesmiths from about 1700; and the Balfours since 1897—have all been intensely concerned with silviculture. Between about 1800 and 1930 the owners supported many of the plant-collecting expeditions mentioned in the following chapter.

Dawyck House stands over 600 feet above sea-level, and the 5,000-acre estate rises to the 1,500-foot line. With an average rainfall of some thirty-five inches, severe gales and very hard frosts, this is a tough environment. The lime-free soil suits plants which thrive in acid conditions, and the Balfours have introduced many rhododendrons, natural species and hybrid forms. The wealth of tree-cover enables shrubs to withstand the gales. The worst ever recorded (134 m.p.h.) occurred in January 1968, when about 50,000 trees were lost.

Dawyck has long been famous for the variety of its trees, which are far too numerous to be detailed here. Colonel A. N. Balfour lent me a list which included twenty-six varieties of pine, twenty-one of fir, seventeen of spruce and the same of maple. The first European larch (north-east of the house) dates from 1725 and is thought to be the oldest in Scotland. The fastigiate Dawyck beech originated here; the original tree may be seen through a yew arch some 250 yards south-east of the house.

In 1897 the grandmother of the present owner purchased the estate, and from that date until his death in

47

1945 her son, F. R. S. Balfour, continued to plant rare species, many collected by himself in North America. The *Picea breweriana* which he lifted in the wild in Oregon in 1908 was lost in 1973, but other examples of this spruce may be seen, easily identified by its deep-green fringe-like foliage.

The lovely stonework—steps, balustrades and vases—which ornaments the garden around the house, was carried out in 1830 by Italian craftsmen imported by the Naesmiths. The same workmen later moved into Kent and made the terraces at Chartwell, home of Sir Winston Churchill. Dawyck also possesses a typical Scottish walled garden, situated a little distance east of the house. Here in summer the visitor is plunged into a riot of roses, honeysuckle, clematis and traditional herbaceous plants, all set round a stone well and protected by yew hedges.

Smaller trees which colour well in autumn are *Prunus sargentii*; the Japanese Katsura tree; *Cornus nuttallii*, a fine Dogwood; and the rare *Disanthus cercidifolia*, which Mr Robert Blair, the head gardener, managed to establish with difficulty. Now nearly thirty years old, it was the first shrub to win an Award of Merit from the Royal Horticultural Society for foliage alone.

Thousands of visitors come to Dawyck every year. A favourite spot with most of them is the glen, a cleft in the rocks with a burn tumbling down from Scrape Hill. The ancient parish church of Dawyck, now a private chapel, will be found half buried in the trees to the right of the house. In spring thousands of bulbs set the woods alight. The late Colonel F. R. S. Balfour obtained from Tresco in Scilly one ton of bulbs every year for twenty years.

The woodlands are being run as a commercial forestry enterprise by Colonel A. N. Balfour. With the exception of beech and sycamore, hardwoods do not grow quickly enough to make them an economic crop to plant. Most of the woodland is composed of conifers introduced from America. He plants not for himself but for his grandchildren. Let us now praise famous men, such as plant trees.

Botanic Gardens and Plant Collectors

THE Edinburgh Royal Botanic Garden is popular today with thousands of visitors. This amenity value to the public is not, however, its primary purpose. It is a centre of botanical research, especially in that branch known as taxonomy, which deals with the accurate identification of plants and their classification, distribution, etc. The Herbarium contains nearly one and a half million specimens, and the Library 45,000 volumes. Although these are not open to everyone, they are available for study and consultation by research workers and interested amateurs.

A booklet called *The Garden Companion*, issued by the Royal Botanic Garden, provides a map and suggestions for touring the grounds; explains the system of labelling plants; and describes ten sections, from the Heather Garden to the Arboretum. Most people put the great Rock Garden high on their list. Yet in 1907 Reginald Farrer, in his book *My Rock Garden*, wrote: 'There are three prevailing plans, none of which is good. The first is what I may call the almond-pudding scheme that obtains generally, especially in the north of England. You take a round bed; you pile it up with soil; you then choose the spikiest pinnacles of limestone you can find, and you insert them quickly with their points in the air, until the general effect is that of a tipsy-cake stuck with almonds. . . . The second style is that of the dog's grave. The pudding shape is more or less the same in both, but the stones are laid flat in the dog's grave ideal. The third style is the Devil's lapful. . . . The finest specimens of this style are to be seen in such gardens as

... Edinburgh. The plan is simplicity itself. You take a hundred or a thousand cartloads of bald square-faced boulders. You next drop them about absolutely anyhow; and you then plant things amongst them. ...'

It may be that the Regius Keeper of that time was influenced by Farrer's criticism. In the following year the existing rock garden was abolished and an entirely new design, of greater boldness and natural effect, gradually took its place. It was not completed until 1914, in a form largely as we know it today. By modern standards there is rather too much rock and not enough soil, but prostrate brooms, junipers and cotoneasters help to disguise the boulders. The general effect is impressive, particularly the generous sweep of the North Scree, with the Heather Garden beyond (see over).

For the amateur gardener, the Peat Garden—a series of raised borders supported by peat turves to produce irregular terraces—supplies useful ideas to be copied or adapted. The best peat for this purpose is cut from the top layer of a deposit. It is open and spongy in texture and can be wetted without trouble. Hard blocks, cut from a deeper layer and intended for use as fuel, are less satisfactory for building peat gardens. Dwarf rhododendrons of creeping, mat-forming habit do well, and help to stabilise the construction. Primulas, dwarf lilies, Ourisias and the even tinier Meconopsis species grow between ericaceous shrubs to form a pleasing picture at most seasons.

Near the pond is a collection of trees and shrubs grown for the attractive colour of their bark, which is at its best in winter and early spring. Here, too, those who are about to make a new garden or refurbish an old one may gain many ideas. There is a fine collection of rhododendrons and azaleas, a number of magnolias and

E   51

North Scree, with Heather Garden beyond, Royal Botanic Garden, Edinburgh

many other shrubs and climbers of great interest out of doors, in addition to the exhibition plant and palm houses.

Since 1969 the Royal Botanic Garden has also taken in charge the well-known collection at Logan, halfway down the Mull of Galloway, the most southerly part of Scotland. It was made by the brothers Kenneth and Douglas McDouall, the last of a very old family who had lived on the estate since the twelfth century.

They spent most of their lives travelling all over the world to collect plants from the warm temperate regions, which they brought back home to Logan and skilfully established. Here may be seen groups of the so-called 'cabbage palm' (see over), a native of New Zealand (and really a member of the lily family); an avenue of the Chusan palm collected by Robert Fortune; various water and tree ferns; huge eucalyptus trees; and such exotics as *Fascicularia bicolor*, the stemless perennial relative of the pineapple, which has great crimson leaves at flowering time, the rosettes of which circle the central blue flower.

The Logan peat garden is a museum-piece, for the McDouall brothers were the first gardeners to make such a construction. It was designed to house the dwarf, high-alpine rhododendrons of Western China and Tibet, and it succeeded very well.

Another annexe to the Royal Botanic Garden is the 100-acre Younger Garden at Benmore in Argyllshire, given to the nation in 1928 by Mr H. G. Younger of Benmore and Kilmun. It consists mainly of woodland garden, and is famous for its rich collection of conifers. The assembly of 'garden conifers' within the Formal Garden is a splendid object-lesson for those who wish to plant them at home, and should help people to avoid the mistake made by my friend, who put in 'two dear little

'Cabbage palms' at Logan Garden

54

deodars' close to her front door.

The double row of Wellingtonias (*Sequoiadendron giganteum*), which form a handsome avenue near the entrance, were planted between 1865 and 1870. They are still growing. When measured in 1973 the tallest had reached 150 feet, and over twenty-one feet in girth. This tree was a supremely fashionable 'status symbol' in the second half of Queen Victoria's reign. Estate owners felt bound to plant one or more of the Californian giants.

In many parts of rural England, also southern Scotland, it is possible to track down a local mansion by spotting the dark conical shapes of Wellingtonias. At Swinton House in Berwickshire Mrs Swinton of Swinton told me that her two huge Wellingtonias—originally put close to the house—grew bigger than expected. They were successfully moved at a fairly advanced stage, and now flourish on a site twenty or thirty yards farther off. William Lobb brought specimens and seed of this tree from America in 1853. It made as much of a sensation as the 'Monkey Puzzle', which Menzies brought home at the end of the eighteenth century.

The Botanic Gardens in Glasgow, established by Royal Charter in 1818, seem to have supplied a number of botanists with a stepping-stone to positions of greater consequence. The first occupant of its Regius Chair of Botany, Robert Graham, exchanged the office for that of Professor of Botany in Edinburgh in 1820. Sir William Hooker succeeded him in Glasgow and greatly improved the small botanic garden and raised its standing. He was knighted while still in Glasgow, and subsequently became Director at Kew. His successor in Glasgow, J. H. Balfour, moved to Edinburgh when Graham retired in 1845.

The glass-house, known as Kibble Palace, has an area

of 23,000 square feet and is one of the largest in Britain. It was removed from the grounds of John Kibble's estate at Coulport, Loch Long, and was opened in Glasgow in 1873. For twenty-one years Kibble had the right to manage concerts and other entertainments in the Palace. It now houses plants from various regions, not fully hardy outdoors in Scotland, grouped according to their native geographical areas.

Under the central dome a unique collection of tree ferns may be seen, most of them from New Zealand and Australia. Growth is very slow. Many of them were planted here as long ago as 1881 and are now only forty-five feet high.

The student of botany and the amateur gardener alike will find plenty to interest them in these fine botanic gardens, which cover forty-two acres. An original exhibit labelled 'What's in a Name?' must be helpful to all those gardeners who express such dislike of 'long Latin names'. When it is explained that *Begonia maculata* has its first (genus) name taken from Michael Begon, a seventeenth-century French botanist, and its second (species) name from the Latin for 'spotted', the seeker after knowledge will look for spotted plants in other places and murmur "*maculata*, I presume".

There is a systemic garden for the aspiring botanist; a most imaginative 'chronological' border showing when the commoner plants were first introduced into Britain—one group for each century from the sixteenth to the twentieth; and a herb garden, containing not only the more usual medicinal and culinary herbs, but also a collection of plants used in dyeing, including the woad (*Isatis tinctoria*) which we associate with the Ancient Britons. The present Curator of this educational and entertaining centre—Mr Eric W. Curtis—is ever ready to assist the inquirer.

David Douglas, the Perthshire-born plant collector, served his apprenticeship in the gardens of the Earl of Mansfield, and then moved for a time to Valleyfield at Dunfermline. While he worked at the Botanic Gardens in Glasgow, his industry attracted the attention of W. J. Hooker. The young Douglas accompanied Hooker on plant-collecting forays into the Scottish Highlands—Hooker was then writing his *Flora Scotica*—and it was he who recommended Douglas as a botanical collector to the London Horticultural Society.

In June 1823, at the age of twenty-four, Douglas left London for New York. His main objective was to gather fruit trees and any other plants and seeds which might be given him in America. He returned in January 1824, to be received with commendation by the Council of the Society, which reported that he had 'obtained many plants which were much wanted, and greatly increased our collection of fruit trees'.

Douglas had found nineteen of the thirty-four species of oak known on the North American continent, and had brought home the Oregon Grape (*Mahonia aquifolium*), a shrub now commonly grown in Britain. In 1824 he undertook a far more ambitious journey, which took him to the north-west coast of America, by way of Rio de Janeiro and Cape Horn. The vessel *William and Mary* had to wait for six weeks to cross the sandbanks at the mouth of the Columbia River, owing to stormy weather, before she was able to anchor in Baker's Bay.

Almost at once Douglas had the first view of the magnificent fir tree which came to be known as the Douglas Fir. For the next three years he travelled through virgin country, braving all kinds of dangers and privations, eventually making his way from Fort Vancouver to Hudson Bay. There the *Prince of Wales* took him on board for the voyage back to Portsmouth, which he reached in October 1827. He brought home a vast collection of seed. To him we owe the popular annual, Clarkia; the Flowering Currant; *Garrya elliptica*; and the *Lupinus polyphyllus* which, crossed with *Lupinus arboreus*, has produced the brilliant strain known as Russell Lupins. The whole expedition cost less than £400.

The third expedition, begun in 1829, ended tragically. Whether he was pushed or fell accidentally is not known, but David Douglas came to a horrible end in a pit in which a bullock had been trapped. The beast gored him to death. This terrible waste of a life still young and full of promise happened in Hawaii, where he was buried. He was thirty-five. In 1841 the people of his birthplace—Scone, in Perthshire—erected an impressive memorial to the famous plant collector.

Douglas's contemporary, Robert Fortune, was born in 1812 in a farm cottage at Blackadder near Chirnside in Berwickshire. His apprentice years were spent in the nearby gardens of Kelloe House, and in 1839 he went to the Royal Botanic Garden, Edinburgh, where he served under the famous William McNab. The latter recommended him for a post at the Chiswick Garden of the London Horticultural Society (which did not become 'Royal' until 1861). He had distinguished himself by gaining a First Class in 1836, at the first examination held by the Society.

In 1842, after the Treaty of Nanking allowed Britain access to several Chinese ports, the Society resolved to send out a plant collector to find out how much plant material from China could usefully be introduced into the United Kingdom. In 1843 Robert Fortune was chosen for the enterprise, and over a period of nineteen years he carried out a number of highly successful journeys. The Society sponsored the first four expeditions. Later, after a term as Curator of the Chelsea Physic Garden, Fortune made several more expeditions under the auspices of the East India Company, with the main purpose of introducing China tea into India.

The briefing given to this young man by the Horticultural Society in 1843 included these words: 'In all cases you will bear in mind that hardy plants are of first importance to the Society, and that the value of the plants diminishes as the heat required to cultivate them is increased. Aquatics, Orchidaceae, or plants producing very handsome flowers are the only exceptions to this rule.'

Fortune was supplied with spade, trowels, hygrometers and thermometers and a 'life preserver'. His request for firearms, at first refused, was later granted. A fowling piece, pistols and a Chinese vocabulary were added to his equipment. According to records preserved by the Society, 'on at least three occasions he had cause to resort to the fowling piece and did so with the greatest composure and competence'.

Chrysanthemums, tree paeonies, the Japanese Cedar, the so-called 'Japanese Anemone' beloved by our grandmothers, several rhododendrons, including the parents of the popular 'Kurume' azaleas, the Chinese snowball tree, Diervilla (or *Weigela florida*), and that favourite plant in the old cottage garden, 'Bleeding Heart', are some of the introductions we owe to him. It is strange now to recall that the Winter Jasmine, so familiar to us as to be commonly regarded as a native of these islands, was brought here from China by Robert Fortune.

In the years immediately preceding the Second

World War, Major George Sherriff and his friend Frank Ludlow made expeditions to Bhutan, south-east Tibet and Kashmir in search of plants. In 1938 they were accompanied by Dr George (now Sir George) Taylor, who later became Director of the Royal Botanic Gardens at Kew, a post he vacated in 1970. Ludlow and Sherriff returned to the same area after the war, and in 1949 sent home by air a bulky collection of living plants—the first time this mode of transport had been used for a large collection. This was Sherriff's last expedition. In 1950 he returned to Scotland for good, and in 1967, in his seventieth year, died at his home, Ascreavie, near Kirriemuir.

Many lovely finds, ranging from rhododendrons to little rock plants, primulas, meconopsis, gentians and lilies, are to be seen today in the garden at Ascreavie, where they are given skilled and devoted care by George Sherriff's widow, Betty. The youngest daughter of the Revd Dr Graham of Kalimpong—who founded the Dr Graham Homes for needy Anglo-Indian children—she married George in 1942 and at once set off on a long trek through the mountains to Lhasa with her husband, who went there to take up a government appointment. After the war she accompanied him on his two last expeditions, and deserves to be remembered as a plant hunter herself.

Volume 174 of the *Botanical Magazine* is dedicated to those lifelong friends, who always spoke to one another simply as 'Ludlow' and 'Sherriff'. No Christian names for them. They are described in its pages as 'knowledgeable and resolute plant collectors, whose rewarding journeys in the eastern Himalaya and in south-eastern Tibet have added greatly to our knowledge of the flora and natural history of these regions, and whose strenuous efforts on hazardous expeditions have enriched our gardens by the introduction of plants of outstanding merit'.

The late John and Dorothy Renton, who from 1922 to 1967 transformed two acres of neglected nursery into a plant-lover's Mecca, might have disclaimed the right of Branklyn to find a place among botanical gardens, for they were as modest as they were talented. Since the death in 1967 of the surviving member of the partnership, John Renton, Branklyn has been administered by The National Trust for Scotland, with assistance from the City of Perth, within whose boundaries the garden is situated. Responsibility for maintaining it has been accepted because the collection is of the most outstanding merit.

Two scree beds, made to the formula suggested by Reginald Farrer, contain treasures, among them the difficult Paraquilegia; near the path grows *Corydalis cashmeriana*, its grey foliage setting off brilliant blue flowers. In late May and June the groups of Meconopsis are a spectacular sight. The delicate 'harebell poppy', the lovely yellow *M.regia*, the differing blues of *M.grandis*★ and *M.betonicifolia*, the tall *M.nepalensis* (some plants bearing red flowers, some pale blue)—the bonus of gold-dusted stems and pods, all at their best in late afternoon sun—alone justify a journey to Perth.

The rainfall here is only some thirty inches a year, and the land, sloping south and west, drains rapidly. This is a very different environment from the 'Gulf Stream' gardens of the west coast; yet the Rentons managed to grow many tender moisture-lovers, such as the Chilean fire bush (*Embothrium coccineum*), whose flaming red blooms in May are also a feature of Inverewe.

★ A fine strain raised here, called 'Branklyn', gained a first-class R.H.S. certificate in 1963.

Branklyn contains a number of interesting trees, including the Chinese birch with copper-coloured bark, a specimen started here from seed in 1926; a ginkgo; a golden cedar; an umbrella pine; a fine weeping Canadian hemlock; and some small, rounded maples (*Acer palmatum dissectum*), which are old inhabitants of this domain. The whole place has a curiously peaceful atmosphere, one of complete seclusion, making it hard to believe that the city of Perth and a heavy flow of traffic encircle it.

A comparative newcomer to the contemporary Scottish gardens scene is the garden at Belhaven near Dunbar, now being re-created by Sir George Taylor. In what is described as a 'very.remarkable micro-climate', many unusual plants given by the Royal Botanic Gardens at Kew and Edinburgh, by Bodnant, the Savill Garden at Windsor and other donors, are now being grown on the coast of East Lothian with marked success. Unexpectedly tender plants of mature age which were found in this garden suggest that at some earlier time there may have been a link with the Edinburgh Botanic Garden.

Sir George Taylor, until 1970 Director at Kew, now supervises Belhaven and acts as Director of the Stanley Smith Horticultural Trust, founded in 1970 to promote world-wide encouragement of horticulture. Grants have been made to such diverse activities as Curtis's *Botanical Magazine*; various plant-collecting expeditions; the rehabilitation of Bogor Botanic Garden in Indonesia; and to the Fairchild Tropical Garden in Florida. Nearer home, the University Botanic Gardens of Dundee and St Andrews have been helped, as has The National Trust for Scotland's horticultural information centre on the outskirts of Edinburgh.

Nurseries and a Gardening School

SCOTLAND has a number of small, specialised nursery gardens, many of them tucked away off the beaten track. The more remote often turn out to be the most rewarding when found. One such is the lovely alpine nursery garden of Aberchalder at Gorthleck in Inverness-shire. It lies in a sheltered glen on the northern edge of the Monadhliath mountains about 800 feet above sea-level. These gardens, belonging to Mrs V. M. Bethell, were originally laid out nearly fifty years ago.

Alpine and bog plants are grown here in profusion around a large pond, sheltered by some fine old trees. Mr Ewen MacDonald, who has worked here for the fifty years of his gardening life, was asked how much help he had. A little sadly he replied that he worked "Often alone". Nevertheless the plants—*Daphne blagayana, D. retusa,* white martagon lilies and *Anemone pulsatilla*—were all very well grown and carefully packed in fulfilment of my order.

Farther south, a short distance from Aviemore with its huge sports complex and provision for skiers, is the well-known Inshriach Alpine Nursery, founded by Jack Drake in 1938. Here amid the magnificent scenery of the Cairngorms visitors are always welcome in business hours, and there is a wide selection of alpine and rock plants and some interesting small trees, such as the yellow-berried sorbus, 'Joseph Rock', a specimen of which I took home with me.

Winters at Inshriach are very severe, so plants which do well in such climatic conditions are justly deemed fully hardy anywhere in Britain. It was unfortunate that this nursery had to close down during the war years, just when it had been built up. In spring 1946, when plans were made for its rehabilitation, it was discovered that many good plants had quietly continued to flourish and increase themselves, untended among a wild collection of weeds. With this nucleus it took less time than had been expected to set the business on its feet again after years of neglect. Jack Drake retired in 1972, and his partner John Lawson is now in charge.

Near Coldingham, in Berwickshire, the Edrom Nurseries are ranged along the banks of a burn and surrounded by woodland, so sheltered that rough winds off the North Sea scarcely gain entry. At this most attractive nursery garden customers may see the plants at home in a natural setting (see opposite). It shares with Inverewe the curious quality of not—apparently—having had the help of human ingenuity in the making. The visitor is bound to wonder if it sprang unaided from the soil, or dropped from the skies of its own volition.

In fact, on the advice of Dr McWatt—an acknowledged authority on European primulas—it was founded in 1925 by two knowledgeable and hardworking sisters, Helen and Edith Logan Home, at their old family residence, Edrom House, not far from Duns. In 1936 the flourishing enterprise was moved to its present site at Silverwells, retaining the original name of Edrom Nurseries.

It is probably unique in Britain, because it propagates and sells plants and seeds developed from specimens collected in the wild by the owners. They made a number of expeditions—into the hills of Kashmir and high alpine regions in Europe—in search of primulas and other plants, all without any fuss or publicity. Like their sister, Mrs Swinton of Swinton, they were first-

Primulas and species rhododendrons at Edrom Nursery, Berwickshire

class plantswomen. Their inventive minds also produced the plant-token scheme which has now become popular everywhere.

Edith died in 1973 and Helen ('Molly') in 1976. The remaining partner, Alex Duguid, is still carrying on. This skilled gardener has received several awards from the Royal Horticultural Society, including the Flora medal in 1973 and the silver Banksian medal in 1969.

At Balbithan House, in a secluded valley two miles north-east of Kintore, Aberdeenshire, Mrs Mary McMurtrie has made a garden splendidly in keeping with her ancient house. She issues a list of surplus plants, those at present on sale being mainly alpines, gentians and heathers. Her little nursery is worth seeing, but visitors are asked to telephone in advance. Balbithan is said to have been built by a laird who wished 'neither Friend nor Foe to find him'. Instructions for finding it will be given when appointments are made. A plant list is available by post.

Scotland is known as the land of heather, and many nurseries supply the various ericas which are now popular garden subjects. The Heather Nursery of Oliver and Hunter at Moniaive, near Thornhill, specialises in these plants and is an attraction for visitors to Dumfriesshire.

Among larger, old-established businesses of nurserymen and seedsmen, Dobbie (Glasgow and Edinburgh), Anderson and Ben Reid (both of Aberdeen), Ferguson (Dunfermline) and Glendoick Gardens, Perth, have world-wide reputations. There are also producers of the 'Scotch' seed potato, which no self-respecting kitchen garden or allotmen can do without.

The Threave Garden at Castle Douglas, Dumfriesshire, where plants may be purchased between

April and October, is far more than a nursery. It is a school of practical gardening, set up in 1957 by The National Trust for Scotland on the estate of the late Major Alan Gordon, who bequeathed his house and land for the purpose.

In the past, many great gardens acted as training grounds for boys who wished to make horticulture their career. Owing to rising costs and labour shortage, few landowners are now in a position to accept trainees. It is for this reason that the plan to make Threave into a training school was conceived.

Residential accommodation has been provided for fourteen students, who stay for a course of two years' duration. On the satisfactory completion of their studies here, these young gardeners are helped to find employment, or additional training at a Botanic Garden. There are no prescribed educational qualifications for entry, but a minimum of one year's practical horticultural experience is necessary.

Threave is more than a training ground. It is a country garden of some sixty-five acres, situated mostly on a western slope about ten miles from the Solway Firth. The garden has been laid out since 1960 on what used to be grass parkland round the Victorian mansion-house, and this work is still going on.

Visitors are welcome. There is much to see, from rose garden and arboretum to a forestry nursery, with an object-lesson in the design of island beds filled with herbaceous plants, meant to be looked at from all sides. For those interested in a current revival of the Victorian culture of ferns, a number are to be seen here in beds constructed with oak logs. There is also an attractive rock garden and a fairly new patio beside the walled garden, demonstrating the use of stone and showing examples of plants suitable for the interstices.

Mr W. R. Hean, the Principal of this school, was asked if many of his ex-students followed the traditional movement of 'Scotch' gardeners down to famous gardens in England. In reply he said that their distribution was now world-wide. There are more ex-students outside Scotland than in it; very few are employed in privately owned gardens. Mr Hean drew attention to the fine collection of dwarf rhododendrons, the latest acquisition at Threave, which the late Sir James Horlick of Achamore, Gigha, bequeathed to The National Trust for Scotland. The larger hybrids from Gigha have been taken to Brodick.

The National Trust for Scotland and Scotland's Gardens Scheme

INFORMATION about all properties owned by The National Trust for Scotland may be obtained from the headquarters at 5 Charlotte Square, Edinburgh EH2 4DU. The Trust formed its Scottish Gardens Committee in 1950, with the late Mary, Lady Elphinstone, D.C.V.O., as its first convener. In 1952 Inverewe was the first property to be taken over by the Trust solely on its merits as a garden.

Scotland's Gardens Scheme, founded in 1931, has raised large sums each year to be shared by the Gardeners' Royal Benevolent Society, the Royal Gardeners Orphan Fund, the Scottish Queen's Nurses Fund and the Gardens Fund of The National Trust for Scotland. From the headquarters of the Scheme at 26 Castle Terrace, Edinburgh EH1 2EL, a booklet *Scotland's Gardens* may be obtained each year in March. It lists some 1,000 dates and times when private gardens are open to the public in aid of the Scheme, and gives details of others, mostly properties of the Trust, which are open more frequently. Both these bodies are registered as charities, and depend on public support. They receive no government grants.

Outwith their widespread net are the 'little' gardens, which have no publicity, but do so much to bestow brightness on the scene in town and country alike. The pure atmosphere enjoyed by a high proportion of Scottish residents has a beneficial effect on plant growth, while the clarity of the light enhances colour in flowers and foliage. In areas of acid, peaty soil there is also a marked deepening of hue in many flowers which are at home in these conditions.

When the late Vita Sackville-West came north from Sissinghurst Castle to Inverewe, she stopped to admire the unusually rich blue of a common little lobelia which had planted itself at the edge of the drive—an incident recorded at the time in my book *Oasis of the North*. It always seems to me that the wild rose native to Scotland's west coast (occasionally *Rosa canina*, oftener *R.tomentosa*) shows a more vivid colour than its relatives in other parts of the north.

The parks of Scotland are necessarily outwith the scope of this book, but most visitors see the admirable display in Princes Street Gardens, Edinburgh; while Aberdeen is famed throughout the land for the floral richness of its public parks, gardens and roadside verges.

Gardeners all over the world have one topic in common—the pests whose depredations have to be faced at home. Among the larger types of marauders, Scotland has some additions seldom found in other parts of Britain. In addition to the commoner crow and pigeon families, pheasant and partridge, rabbit, mole and grey squirrel, Highland gardeners sometimes have to reckon with black game, brown and blue hares, red squirrels, roe and red deer.

To the dismay of naturalists, the beautiful little pine marten (known in the past as 'Sweet Mart' to distinguish it from the malodorous polecat, or 'Fou' Mart'), has become scarcer than of yore. Gardeners may feel less regretful. Osgood Mackenzie's uncle told him of an incident which occurred over a century ago in the old family garden (*Tigh Dige*) at Gairloch, where a fine

crop of magnum bonum plums was rapidly dis-
appearing from a south wall. The irate gardener covered
this ripe fruit with several folds of herring-net, and in it
caught a large marten, which he shot. Its belly was
found to be stuffed full of the yellow plums—but it had
been clever enough to leave the stones in heaps on top of
the wall.

Pests and predators are only one facet of the hazards
which Scottish gardeners have to contend with. My own
experience, with a post-war background of gardening in
lush Somerset country, followed by a spell in the particularly mild, moist climate of Wester Ross at
Inverewe, left me ill-prepared for later work in the
Scottish Borders.

In Berwickshire I planted a cottage garden, happily
assuming that I knew enough to carry it through without trouble. Soon I discovered that even the common
runner bean had become a difficult subject. Drying and
bitter winds from the North Sea often persisted through
the month of May, and began again when plants were
still bearing, cutting the late starters down almost in
their prime. In the same garden I went so far as to stake
brussels sprouts and broccoli to keep them from heeling
over, with roots torn out of the light soil, during fierce
and prolonged winter gales.

The Scots gardener, who must learn from the start to
deal with tough conditions, used to be hardened off
himself in youth with long walks in all weathers to
school, backed up by spartan living at home. Older
people in the Highlands now shake their heads. What
with bus and taxi transport provided by the State for
schoolchildren in rural areas, and constant expenditure
on sweets and pastries, the nation's strength is bound to
suffer, they say. In their view, footslogging on a diet of

oatmeal and salt herring produced greater physical and mental stamina. Time will show.

These pages deal solely with past and present, leaving others to peer into the future. Enough has been said to demonstrate that the Scots gardener of today possesses a full share of the skill, wisdom and energy for which his forebears were so justly renowned.

Reading List

Arboretum Britannicum, J. C. Loudon.
Carefree Gardening, Margery Fish.
Cottage Garden Flowers, Margery Fish.
Discovering Period Gardens, John Anthony.
The English Rock Garden, Reginald Farrer.
Flowers and their Histories, Alice M. Coats.
Garden Shrubs and their Histories, Alice M. Coats.
Gardening in Britain, Miles Hadfield.
The Gardens of Scotland, Peter Verney.
Gleanings in Old Garden Literature, W. C. Hazlitt.
Herbs and the Fragrant Garden, Margaret Brownlow.
A History of Gardening in Scotland, E. H. M. Cox.
A Hundred Years in the Highlands, Osgood Mackenzie.
A Modern Herbal, Mrs M. Grieve.
Oasis of the North (Inverewe), Dawn MacLeod.
On the Making of Gardens, Sir George Sitwell.
A Prospect of Flowers, Andrew Young.
Scots Gardens in Olden Times, Elizabeth Haldane.
The Scots Gard'ner, John Reid.
Scottish Gardens, Sir Herbert Maxwell.
V. Sackville-West's Garden Book.
The Speaking Garden, Edward Hyams.
We Made a Garden, Margery Fish.